THE
BALANCE SHEET
POCKETBOOK

By Anne Hawkins and Clive Turner

Drawings by Phil Hailstone

"A uniquely accessible guide - if you only read one book on finance, read this!"
Peter Colley, Director of Finance and Membership Services,
RAC Motoring Services Ltd

"The authors' wealth of practical experience and understanding of the line manager's perspective is fully reflected in this clear and readable book."
Ray Jennings, Human Resources Director, Dowty Aerospace

CONTENTS

 This symbol refers the reader back to a previous section where the item or term has already been explained

INTRODUCTION

CONFUSED?

Reserves

Fixed Assets

Working Capital

Earnings

Capital Employed

Creditors

Debtors

Depreciation

Many people are discouraged in their attempts to understand financial statements by the jargon accountants use ... and a fear of numbers!

INTRODUCTION

DON'T BE PUT OFF!

Use the Structured process:

Step One: Develop a 'common sense' model of business finance

Step Two: Understand the impact of capital and revenue expenditure on this
               Business Financial Model

Step Three: Extract from this Model the
               - Balance Sheet
               - Profit and Loss Account

INTRODUCTION

COMMON MISCONCEPTIONS

Listed below are some of the more common misconceptions we, the authors, encounter in our training sessions. See if any of them seem familiar ...

- ◆ *'The Balance Sheet tells me the value of the business'*

- ◆ *'At the year-end the retained profit must be somewhere; in the bank, or the accountant's drawer'*

- ◆ *'If the company's share price rises it has more money'*

- ◆ *'If I compare the results of two businesses, the one which has made more profit has done better'*

- ◆ *'The accountant balances the Balance Sheet by entering a balancing figure somewhere ... probably profit'*

These misconceptions will be dealt with at appropriate points in the book.

THE BUSINESS FINANCIAL MODEL

THE BUSINESS FINANCIAL MODEL

INTRODUCTION

In this section a Business Model is developed which explains in straightforward terms how money works within the business.

THE BUSINESS FINANCIAL MODEL

THE MODEL

SHARE CAPITAL	LOAN CAPITAL	RETAINED PROFITS

SOURCE OF FUNDS

USE OF FUNDS

FACILITIES / PROCESSES	PRODUCTS / SERVICES
FIXED ASSETS	WORKING CAPITAL

Sales

Less: Attributable Cost

Operating Profit

Less: Interest

Less: Tax

Earnings

Depreciation

Dividend	Retained Profits

THE BUSINESS FINANCIAL MODEL

APPLYING THE MODEL

Use the model to understand **your** business

- How is **your** business funded?
- What have **you** used this money for?
- How much profit do **you** make?
- **IS IT WORTH THE EFFORT?**

Make the Business Model and Financial Reports work for you!

Let's start at the beginning ———————➤

THE BUSINESS FINANCIAL MODEL

SOURCE OF FUNDS

Most businesses need **long-term finance**, ie: money that is being invested in the business on a long-term basis, to allow it to achieve its aims.

There are three categories of long-term finance:

- Share capital

- Loan capital

- Retained profits

Each of these has different investor expectations and implications for the way the business is run.

Most companies will choose to have a mix of the three types.

THE BUSINESS FINANCIAL MODEL

SOURCE OF FUNDS

SHARE CAPITAL

Definition:

Individuals or financial institutions provide capital by buying shares in the business.
They do this in anticipation of a return comprising:
- dividends
- growth

Dividends:

- Generally paid twice a year - an interim dividend based on the half-year accounts - a final dividend dependent on the full year's result

- No legal obligation for the company to pay a dividend

Growth:

- The investment increases in value, creating the opportunity to sell at a profit

THE BUSINESS FINANCIAL MODEL

SOURCE OF FUNDS

IMPLICATIONS OF SHARE CAPITAL

- The shareholders own the business, **not** the Chief Executive and Board of Directors

- Shareholder expectations, therefore, have to be treated with respect

- If the performance of the business does not meet shareholder expectations:

    - some or all of the Board may be dismissed
    - investors may sell their shares, leading to a fall in share prices, thus
    - making the business vulnerable to being `taken over'

Note   To acquire the business a predator has to buy the **shares**, not the land, buildings, stock, etc. If the share price falls, the business becomes cheaper to buy.

THE BUSINESS FINANCIAL MODEL

COMMON MISCONCEPTIONS

'If the company's share price rises it has more money. If it falls, it has less.'

Apart from when the company wishes to raise new share capital or is warding off a takeover bid, the share price has no immediate impact on the business.

Example: Alex invests £1,000 in the shares of a new business.
The company receives £1,000 which it uses to buy stock and machinery. Alex receives a piece of paper ... a Share Certificate.

When the company prospers, Bill offers to buy the shares for £1,200. Alex hands over the piece of paper; Bill hands over the £1,200.

Alex has made a gain of £200. The company has no involvement in the transaction and its finances are therefore unaffected. Similarly, if the share value falls and Bill decides to sell, he will lose out but there will be no effect on the company accounts.

THE BUSINESS FINANCIAL MODEL

SOURCE OF FUNDS

LOAN CAPITAL

Definition:

Money on loan to the business which will have to be repaid

- The first thing any potential lender will want to see is the Business Plan

- Having satisfied himself that the proposed venture is viable, the lender will require
  - interest on the loan
  - eventual repayment of the loan itself

- The terms of the loan will be defined by a contractual agreement

THE BUSINESS FINANCIAL MODEL

SOURCE OF FUNDS

IMPLICATIONS OF LOAN CAPITAL

Borrowing money, ie: loan capital, entails financial risk

- The terms of the loan are defined by contractual agreement

- The business has to keep making the payments of Interest and Capital, whether or not it is trading profitably

- The lender will require **security** or collateral (so that the loan can be recovered if the borrower defaults)

THE BUSINESS FINANCIAL MODEL

SOURCE OF FUNDS
LOAN CAPITAL - EXAMPLE

Taking out a mortgage is a similar process to a business loan:

1   The lender considers the **'business plan'**

    ● The real value of the property

    ● How much you wish to borrow

    ● Your income and existing outgoings

2   The **mortgage agreement** defines the terms of the loan

3   As **security,** the lender retains the title deeds in case you default on your payments

THE BUSINESS FINANCIAL MODEL

SOURCE OF FUNDS
RETAINED PROFITS

Definition:

When a business makes 'profits' it has the opportunity to plough back some of the money it has made to self-finance its future growth.

- Retained profit is money the business has made itself

- It is therefore the cheapest source of long-term finance avoiding:
  - dividend payments
  - interest payments

Hence the company financing a larger proportion of its business
with Retained Profits has a

COMPETITIVE ADVANTAGE

THE BUSINESS FINANCIAL MODEL

SOURCE OF FUNDS

SUMMARY

Summary of the categories of Long-term Finance:

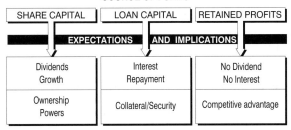

SOURCE OF FUNDS

SHARE CAPITAL	LOAN CAPITAL	RETAINED PROFITS
EXPECTATIONS AND IMPLICATIONS		
Dividends Growth	Interest Repayment	No Dividend No Interest
Ownership Powers	Collateral/Security	Competitive advantage

THE BUSINESS FINANCIAL MODEL

USE OF FUNDS

A business raises Long-term Funds in order
to spend it on things required
to run the business:

SHOPPING LIST

Premises
Materials
Labour
Machines
Utilities
Insurance
Vehicles
Maintenance
Computers

THE BUSINESS FINANCIAL MODEL

USE OF FUNDS

Items on the shopping list are grouped to reflect the nature and significance of the expenditure:

	Facilities/Processes Tools to do the job **... to be used!**	Products/Services Materials and added value **... to be sold!**
	eg: Premises Machines Vehicles Computers	eg: Materials Labour Utilities Insurance Maintenance
TIMESCALE:	Retain for many years	Continually changing
SCALE:	High Value Items	Low Value Items
DECISION LEVEL:	Strategic	Operational
ACCOUNTANT'S JARGON:	Fixed Assets	Working Capital

THE BUSINESS FINANCIAL MODEL

USE OF FUNDS

FACILITIES/PROCESSES - FIXED ASSETS

Facilities and processes ....tools to do the job, to be used

How much investment do you need? This will depend on:

- Nature and scale of business
- Type of industry
- Service provided to customer

Business Position		Process Investment
Retailing		High Street outlets or out-of-town stores? What about warehousing and transport?
Distribution		Transport What about warehousing?
Manufacturer		Plant and machinery What about warehousing and transport?

THE BUSINESS FINANCIAL MODEL

USE OF FUNDS

PRODUCTS/SERVICES - WORKING CAPITAL

Products and services ... for sale to the customer

Funds are required to provide the flow of materials, services and credit to achieve the sales and satisfy customer needs. Accountants call this **working capital**... and that is exactly what the investment has to do ... **WORK!**

- Cash is used to buy
- Raw Materials, which are converted into
- Work in Progress, and through to
- Finished Goods, which are then
- Sold to customers,
- Who, after the agreed credit period, pay for the goods they have received

This process is referred to as the   CURRENT ASSET CYCLE
Note: Stock = Raw Materials + Work in Progress + Finished Goods

THE BUSINESS FINANCIAL MODEL

USE OF FUNDS

WORKING CAPITAL: CREDIT

- Most businesses do not receive cash on delivery from their customers or pay cash on delivery to their suppliers

- Credit is allowed to customers and taken from suppliers

  Debtors - the amount owed by customers for goods they have received
  - customers are 'indebted' to the business
  - also referred to as 'Receivables'
  - part of **Current Assets** p21

  Creditors - the amount owed to suppliers for goods/services received but not yet paid for
  - also referred to as 'Payables'
  - part of **Current Liabilities** (ie: short-term owings)

THE BUSINESS FINANCIAL MODEL

USE OF FUNDS

WORKING CAPITAL CYCLE

The Working Capital
cycle can then
be shown as:

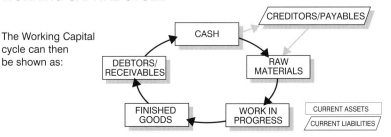

How much has the business invested in Working Capital?

- Not all the stock will have been paid for. Therefore Working Capital is the value of
  Current Assets less the amount owed to suppliers:

  WORKING CAPITAL = CURRENT ASSETS *less* CURRENT LIABILITIES
  $\qquad\qquad\qquad\quad$ = (STOCK *plus* DEBTORS *plus* CASH) *less* CREDITORS

THE BUSINESS FINANCIAL MODEL

USE OF FUNDS
WORKING CAPITAL CYCLE

Note

1 The amount of working capital required is a function of:

- The size of the business
- Credit given and taken
- Lead time through the manufacturing process
- Range of products/services offered

2 Moving from cash to other parts of the cycle **entails risk** and must therefore offer the prospect of a **sufficient return** to compensate for such risk

THE BUSINESS FINANCIAL MODEL

USE OF FUNDS

WORKING CAPITAL CYCLE

3 If the goods are being produced at a profit, the business generates profit and cash every time the cycle is completed. Note however that Profit and Cash are measured at different points in the cycle.

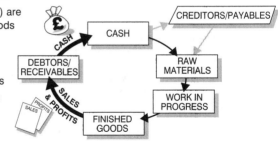

- **Sales** (and hence Profit) are measured when the goods are despatched to the customer

- **Cash** is only received when the customer pays

- This timing difference is one of the factors contributing to the outcome that PROFIT $\neq$ CASH

These ideas are developed in *The Managing Cashflow Pocketbook*

THE BUSINESS FINANCIAL MODEL

SUMMARY

The model so far:

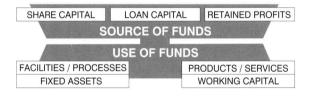

SHARE CAPITAL   LOAN CAPITAL   RETAINED PROFITS

SOURCE OF FUNDS

USE OF FUNDS

FACILITIES / PROCESSES   PRODUCTS / SERVICES
FIXED ASSETS   WORKING CAPITAL

THE BUSINESS FINANCIAL MODEL

DON'T WASTE MONEY

Grasp the significance of this simple model!

Money is raised ...

> SOURCE OF FUNDS

         ... to be used in the business...

> USE OF FUNDS

Every £1 of investment has to be   - **Raised**
                                       - **Financed** (interest and/or dividends paid)

So it is essential to:

- Control Expenditure   - Justify New Processes   - Plan and Control Products

THE BUSINESS FINANCIAL MODEL

MAKING PROFIT

PRODUCTS / SERVICES
WORKING CAPITAL
Sales
Less: Attributable Cost
Operating Profit

- The reason for setting up a business is to generate a profit

- Profit results from sales

- Profit is assessed when the Finished Goods are sold to the customer

- Operating Profit is achieved when the selling price exceeds the attributable costs, ie: the operational costs incurred in sourcing/manufacturing, selling and distributing the goods sold

THE BUSINESS FINANCIAL MODEL

MAKING PROFIT

DEPRECIATION

However, there is something missing.

Companies invest in Fixed Assets in order to provide a facility within which products can be made.

Therefore, part of the cost of the product is a charge for the use of these processes and facilities. This charge is called **DEPRECIATION.**

Note *For the calculation of Depreciation refer to pages 101-106*

THE BUSINESS FINANCIAL MODEL

MAKING PROFIT

OTHER CHARGES TO BE MET

FACILITIES / PROCESSES
FIXED ASSETS

PRODUCTS / SERVICES
WORKING CAPITAL

Depreciation

Sales

Less: Attributable Cost

Operating Profit

Less: Interest

Less: Tax

Earnings

Dividend   Retained Profits

- **Operating Profit:** (often referred to as PBIT - Profit Before Interest and Tax) is used to pay:
  - **interest** to the lenders of Loan Capital p13
  - **tax** to the Government

- **Earnings:** whatever remains after all these costs have been met belongs to the shareholders and will either be:
  - paid out as a **Dividend**, or
  - ploughed back as **Retained Profit** p16

THE BUSINESS FINANCIAL MODEL

THE COMPLETE PICTURE

SHARE CAPITAL	LOAN CAPITAL	RETAINED PROFITS

SOURCE OF FUNDS

USE OF FUNDS

FACILITIES / PROCESSES	PRODUCTS / SERVICES
FIXED ASSETS	WORKING CAPITAL

Depreciation

Sales

Less: Attributable Cost

Operating Profit

Less: Interest

Less: Tax

Earnings

Dividend	Retained Profits

THE BUSINESS FINANCIAL MODEL

OVERVIEW

SOURCE OF FUNDS
- Funds are raised to finance the long-term business requirements

USE OF FUNDS
- Managers choose how to invest the money to:
  - provide the tools to do the job
  - finance the day-to-day running of the business products and services

OPERATING PROFIT
- Products are sold at a profit (or loss)

EARNINGS
- Earnings are distributed as dividends and/or ploughed back as Retained Profit

RETAINED PROFIT
- Retained Profit can be used to finance the purchase of even better facilities and/or an increased product range which would:
  - → increase operating profits
  - → increase Earnings
  - → increase Dividends
  - → retain additional profit... and so the process continues

THE BUSINESS FINANCIAL MODEL

COMMON MISCONCEPTIONS

'At the year-end the Retained Profit must be somewhere; in the bank, or the accountant's drawer.'

*Yes. The Retained Profit **is** somewhere - it has been re-invested back within the business. If the company merely 'collected' Retained Profit and held it until the year-end before tipping it back into the top of the model, it would be extremely inefficient. This re-cycling is, therefore, happening continuously, ie: there is no tank at the bottom of the model, simply a meter and a pump. Every year the meter is set to zero and the profits are measured as they are re-cycled.*

NOTES

CLASSIFICATION OF EXPENDITURE

CAPITAL or REVENUE?

CLASSIFICATION OF EXPENDITURE

WHY CLASSIFY?

Whenever the business
spends money it
has an impact on
the model.

Expenditure must therefore be:

- Classified - in order for it to be reported correctly within the structure of the model

- Controlled - to ensure it is effective in working the model to achieve the
business financial objectives

CLASSIFICATION OF EXPENDITURE

CAPITAL OR REVENUE?

Capital Expenditure - the purchase/improvement of Fixed Assets ◄◄▌ p20

Revenue Expenditure - expenditure to source, make, sell and deliver the products/services required by the customer

Think of a garage owner with bills to pay for:

● A new recovery vehicle

● An extension to his workshop

● His mechanic's wages

● Some new cars to sell

The first two items are capital expenditure, the second two are revenue.

CLASSIFICATION OF EXPENDITURE

WHAT WILL IT DO TO MY PROFIT?

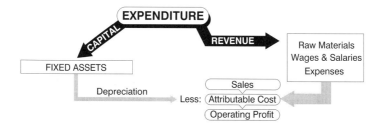

- The impact of Capital Expenditure on Profit is spread over the asset life via the depreciation charge (see page 49)

- Revenue Expenditure is included in Attributable Cost - and hence reduces profit - as soon as the product/service for which it was purchased is sold

CLASSIFICATION OF EXPENDITURE

CONTROL

CAPITAL EXPENDITURE

- Commits Long-Term Finance into processes and facilities to be used over a long period of time

- If your business buys the wrong 'tools'

    - can you get your money back?

    - what if the competition buys better 'tools' - how can you compete?

- Therefore capital expenditure must be supported by a justification - a business plan which examines risk, investment and return

CLASSIFICATION OF EXPENDITURE

CONTROL

REVENUE EXPENDITURE

- Businesses have limited resources
- Plans have to be made and resources allocated to the activities and expenditures required to meet the business aims
- Actual expenditure is compared with planned expenditure to identify any differences (variances)
- Action must then be taken either to:
  - i) bring expenditure back in line with budget, or   ii) amend the budget

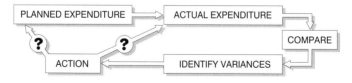

See further *The Managing Budgets Pocketbook*

FINANCIAL REPORTS

INTRODUCTION

Here is the Business Financial Model as developed in the first section of the pocketbook. ◀▮▮ p31

BUSINESS FINANCIAL MODEL

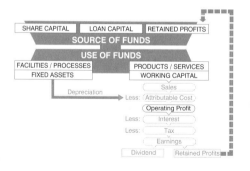

- **Funds are raised** to finance the planned investment

- **Funds are used** in support of the Business Plan

- **Assessment of Profit Performance** - a measure of the effectiveness with which this investment has been used in order to generate profits

FINANCIAL REPORTS

INTRODUCTION

The business must provide information in the form of financial reports to the owners - the shareholders.

These reports include:

i) a summary of the business investment

   ... **a Balance Sheet**

ii) a summary of the operating performance

   ... **the Profit and Loss Account**

INTRODUCTION

The Balance Sheet and Profit and Loss Account are reports of the Business Financial Model:

THE LINK TO THE BUSINESS FINANCIAL MODEL

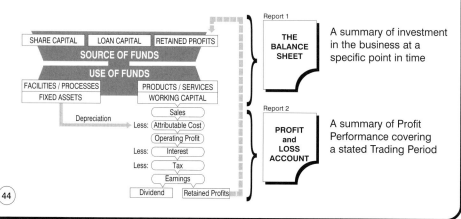

Report 1

THE BALANCE SHEET

A summary of investment in the business at a specific point in time

Report 2

PROFIT and LOSS ACCOUNT

A summary of Profit Performance covering a stated Trading Period

SECTION 1
THE BALANCE SHEET

THE BALANCE SHEET

INTRODUCTION

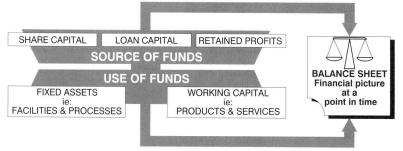

The Balance Sheet is:

- A financial statement of the business investment as at a specific point in time; and
- Reports at the specific point in time
    - where the money invested in the business came from   SOURCE OF FUNDS
    - and how it is currently invested   USE OF FUNDS

THE BALANCE SHEET

FORMAT

The Balance Sheet format swops the two halves of the model over:

- Use of Funds appears at the top of the statement
- Source of Funds appears at the bottom of the statement

Hence ...

Balance Sheet: ARC plc as at 31st December 200-

£

Use of Funds

Fixed Assets
Working Capital

_____

_____

Source of Funds

Share Capital
Retained Profits
Loan Capital

_____

_____

THE BALANCE SHEET

FIXED ASSETS
VALUATION OF FIXED ASSETS

Fixed Assets are:

Facilities and Processes acquired for use in the business as a result of Capital Expenditure p20

Fixed Assets are valued on the Balance Sheet at

	£
Cost, to include:	
purchase costs	
legal costs	
installation costs	
Less:	
Depreciation	_____
ie:	
Net Book Value	
(or Written Down Value)	_____

THE BALANCE SHEET

FIXED ASSETS

DEPRECIATION OF FIXED ASSETS

By definition:

- Fixed Assets are used in the business for a period in excess of one year

- The cost of the Fixed Asset is considered significant given the scale of the business operation

Charging capital expenditure against profits in the year of purchase would **unfairly penalise that year's result** and subsequent years, when the facility continued to be used, would not bear any of the cost.

Therefore there needs to be a basis for apportioning the cost of the investment over the years which will benefit from its use.

The resultant charge is called:

DEPRECIATION

DEPRECIATION OF FIXED ASSETS

Depreciation is not applied to land (with the exception of quarries and mines).

It is applied to
all other Fixed Assets:

WORKING CAPITAL

DEFINITION

The Funds used to provide the flow of materials, services and credit required to achieve the sales and satisfy customer needs.  p23

- Stock (Raw materials,
  Work in Progress and
  Finished Goods)

- Debtors/Receivables
  (Amounts owed by customers)

- Cash

Less:

- Creditors/Payables
  (Amounts owed to suppliers)

Equals Working Capital

CURRENT
ASSETS

CURRENT
LIABILITIES

51

THE BALANCE SHEET

VALUATION OF WORKING CAPITAL

The values shown in the Balance Sheet are as follows:

| Stock | At the **lower** of cost and net realisable (ie: saleable) value
- Allowances are made for slow-moving
  and redundant stock, etc |

| Debtors | At the sum expected to be collected
- Bad debts are written off
- Allowances are made for possible bad debts |

| Cash | At face value |

| Creditors | At the sum expected to be paid |

THE BALANCE SHEET

SOURCE OF FUNDS

VALUATION

We now reach the bottom half of the Balance Sheet, which shows where the funds
(used in the top half) came from.

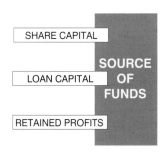

- SHARE CAPITAL
  the number of shares issued valued at
  a standard or 'nominal' value (see page 54)

- LOAN CAPITAL
  long-term borrowings from Banks
  (or similar institutions)

- RETAINED PROFITS
  the accumulation of profits re-invested
  into the business, reported on the
  Balance Sheet under the collective term
  'Reserves' (see page 54)

THE BALANCE SHEET

RESERVES

'Reserves' is a collective term used on the Balance Sheet and forms part of the shareholders' investment in the business.

The principal reserves are:

Retained Profits:
This represents the cumulative profits made by the business which have been 'ploughed back'. ◄◄❶ p16

Share Premium Account:
Share Capital is shown on the Balance Sheet at its 'Nominal Value', eg: £1 per share. If shares are issued above nominal value the premiums are put into the Share Premium Account.

Example: Company X has shares with a nominal value of £1. The company issues 100,000 new shares at the current market price of £1.30.

    Share Capital increases by £100,000
    Share Premium Account increases by £30,000
    balanced by the increase in Cash of £130,000.

THE BALANCE SHEET

RESERVES

Revaluation Reserve:

Companies are required periodically to revalue their Land and Buildings and adjust their Balance Sheet values accordingly.

- The business belongs to the shareholders
- Therefore any change in the value of assets held by the business falls to those shareholders
- Hence any increases or decreases in asset values caused by revaluation will be matched by an increase or decrease in the Revaluation Reserve

Note: Depreciation of Buildings will be based on the revalued amount.

THE BALANCING ACT

- **You can't do something with money you never had**

- **Neither can money you have had just disappear!**

THE BALANCE SHEET

COMMON MISCONCEPTIONS

'The accountant balances the Balance Sheet by entering a balancing figure somewhere ... probably profit.'

The Balance Sheet balances automatically because for every transaction in the books of account there are always two entries - double-entry book-keeping!

The two entries will either increase or decrease both halves of the Balance Sheet by the same amount, or there will be equal plus and minus entries within the same half.

See the following examples.

THE BALANCE SHEET

COMMON MISCONCEPTIONS
EXAMPLES

	Source of Funds	*Use of Funds*
Issue £1m shares (at nominal value) for cash	+ £1m Share Capital	+ £1m Cash
Repay £0.5m Loan Capital	- £0.5m Loan Capital	- £0.5m Cash
Purchase new machine for £50k cash	+ £50k Fixed Asset	- £50k Cash

Remember: *the Balance Sheet **must** balance because the two halves are explaining:*

Source of Funds - *where the money came from*

Use of Funds - *where it is now*

ARC plc

THE
BALANCE
SHEET

THE BALANCE SHEET

SUMMARY

This is a summarised Balance Sheet for ARC plc:

Balance Sheet as at 31st December 200-			
	Note	£`000	£`000
USE OF FUNDS			
Fixed Assets			470
Current Assets		520	
Less:			
Current Liabilities		<u>290</u>	
Working Capital	2		<u>230</u>
Net Assets Employed	1		<u>700</u>
SOURCE OF FUNDS			
Issued Share Capital		300	
Reserves	3	<u>200</u>	
Shareholders' Funds	4		500
Loan Capital			
Net Capital Employed	1		<u>200</u>
			<u>700</u>

THE BALANCE SHEET

SUMMARY

Notes:

1   **Net Assets Employed** is the accountant's term for the total Use of Funds
    Net Capital Employed is the accountant's term for the total Source of Funds
    Hence:
    Net Assets Employed = Net Capital Employed   ◀◀❚❚ p56

2   **Working Capital = Current Assets - Current Liabilities**   ◀◀❚❚ p51

3   **Reserves** is a collective term which includes
    Retained Profits accumulated over the life of the business   ◀◀❚❚ p54

4   **Shareholders Funds** (or Net Worth) is the total amount of long-term funding
    invested by the shareholders either directly (by buying shares) or indirectly
    (by allowing some of their earnings to be re-invested as Retained Profits)

THE BALANCE SHEET

SUMMARY

Here is the same Balance Sheet expanded to itemise the Fixed Assets
and the constituent parts of Working Capital:

Balance Sheet as at 31st December 200-			
	£'000	£'000	£'000
Fixed Assets			
Land & Buildings		230	
Plant & Equipment		170	
Vehicles		70	470
Current Assets			
Stock	320		
Debtors	190		
Cash	10		
Less:			
Current Liabilities		520	
Creditors	290		
		290	
Working Capital			230
Net Assets Employed			700
Source of Funds			
Issued Share Capital			
300,000 £1 Ordinary Shares		300	
Reserves			
Retained Profits		200	
Shareholders Funds			500
Loan Capital			200
Net Capital Employed			700

SUMMARY

Be careful! This statement has its limitations!

Remember that the Balance Sheet is a snapshot, at a point in time, of where the money came from and how it is currently invested.

What do people do before having their photographs taken? They make themselves look as presentable as possible.

Companies do the same thing!

The camera may not lie ... but just what does that business look like for the other 364 days of the year?

Chaotic? - perhaps!

THE BALANCE SHEET

COMMON MISCONCEPTIONS

'The Balance Sheet tells me the value of the business.'

No. Remember the shareholders own the business and therefore the value of the business is the cost of acquiring those shares, ie:

Number of shares x Share Price

There are many reasons why this is not the same as the Balance Sheet value of Shareholders' Funds. For instance, some of the business's value does not appear on the Balance Sheet, eg:

- *Employee skills*
- *Market Opportunities*
- *Order Book*
- *Market value of Fixed Assets or Stocks*

THE BALANCE SHEET

INTERNAL FORMAT

- The format examined to this point has addressed an **internal** report to the Management Team

- The focus has been to consider the Management decisions in respect of the:

    Use of Funds (Net Assets Employed)

  made available to the business from a number of external sources:

    Source of Funds (Net Capital Employed)

- Management must account for and make a return on the Net Capital Employed

- **The Report provides essential management information**

THE BALANCE SHEET

PUBLISHED FORMAT

The Balance Sheet

... published format

A Report to the Owners of the Business

... the Shareholders

- The published format is structured to feature the different needs of the Shareholders - the owners of the business

- The Shareholder is seeking to trace that part of the business funded by the Shareholders either through Share Capital or Reserves

- **This change of end user requires a change of format only.** The accounting terms used to this point are retained with the same definitions

THE BALANCE SHEET

REPORTS TO THE SHAREHOLDERS

Internal Format		£'000	Published Format		£'000
Fixed Assets		470	**Fixed Assets**		470
Current Assets	520		Current Assets	520	
Less:			Less:		
Current Liabilities	290		Current Liabilities	290	
			Net Current Assets		230
Working Capital		230	(Working Capital)		
			Total Assets less		
Net Assets Employed		700	**Current Liabilities**		700
			Less:		
			Creditors/Loans		
			(greater than 1 year)		200
			Total Net Assets		500
Financed by:			Capital and Reserves		
Share Capital		300	Share Capital		300
Reserves		200	Reserves		200
Shareholders' Funds		500	**Shareholders' Funds**		500
Loan Capital		200			
Net Capital Employed		700			

THE BALANCE SHEET

PUBLISHED FORMAT

- In most companies the Balance Sheet is subject to external audit
  (Note: different rules now apply for small companies)

- Current Liabilities includes all items due for payment within the next financial year

- Creditors and Loans (greater than one year) includes items of indebtedness
  required to be paid in the future but not in the next 12 months

- The format provides summary information only - the report is supported with
  detailed notes cross referenced to the Balance Sheet

- The format is required to show the comparative figures for the preceding year

SECTION 2
THE PROFIT AND LOSS ACCOUNT

PROFIT AND LOSS ACCOUNT

LINK BETWEEN FINANCIAL REPORTS

- Revenue performance is assessed in respect of a defined trading period
- The Balance Sheet provides a picture of the business investment **at a specific point in time,** eg:
    - at the start of the trading period
    - and at the end of the trading period
- The Profit and Loss Account reports what happened, in terms of Revenue Performance, between those Balance Sheet dates

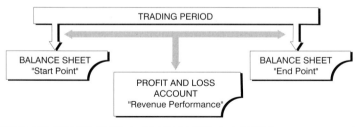

PROFIT AND LOSS ACCOUNT

DIFFERENT APPROACHES

Companies use many different formats and styles to report their revenue or profit
performance internally, eg:

- Trading Account
- Operating Statement
- Revenue Account, etc

Whatever the name, the statement will be reporting on some or all of this part
of the business model.

◀◀▮ p44

PROFIT AND LOSS ACCOUNT

REVENUE PERFORMANCE

Hence the Profit and Loss Account is a statement of revenue performance over a given period of time showing:

- The value of products or services sold - **Sales**

- The costs the business has incurred in meeting those sales

PROFIT AND LOSS ACCOUNT

PROFIT NOT CASH

The Profit and Loss Account measures the profit or loss made on the goods sold during the period.

- It does **not** measure the cashflows into and out of the business

- This is an essential difference

- Cashflow is a vital part of the financial management of the business and is dealt with separately in the Cashflow Statement
  (see further The Managing Cashflow Pocketbook)

- To manage a business both **Profit** and **Cash** must be considered

PROFIT AND LOSS ACCOUNT

PROFIT NOT CASH

SALES

This is the value of product or
services sold during the period
(excluding Value Added Tax)

NOT

the amount of cash collected

(Any sales not yet paid for by
the customer will appear on the
Balance Sheet as Debtors/Receivables.)

PROFIT NOT CASH

ATTRIBUTABLE COSTS

For `Profit' to be a meaningful measure, 'like' has
to be compared with `like'.

DON'T SELL APPLES AND COST PEARS!

Hence Attributable Costs are the
operating costs associated with
producing and delivering the
items sold during the period

NOT
the amount of cash spent

PROFIT AND LOSS ACCOUNT

PROFIT NOT CASH

- Goods received, and not yet used for the products that have been sold will appear as **Stock** on the Balance Sheet

- Goods received, but not yet paid for will appear under **Creditors/Payables** on the Balance Sheet

Example

£100 worth of stock is delivered to your premises

- When it is received: Stock increases by £100   Does not affect
       Creditors increase by £100   profit and loss

- When it is paid for: Creditors decrease by £100   Does not affect
       Cash decreases by £100   profit and loss

- When it is despatched   Stock decreases by £100   Affects profit
  to the customer: Attributable cost increases by £100   and loss NOW

PROFIT AND LOSS ACCOUNT

PROFIT IS NOT CASH

It is evident, therefore, that whenever a business:

● Holds stock, or

● Gives credit, or

● Takes credit

then profit and cash will not be the same thing.

This debate is examined in more detail in *The Managing Cashflow Pocketbook*.

PROFIT AND LOSS ACCOUNT

OPERATING PROFIT

Profit is measured at various levels down the Statement as additional aspects of business cost are taken into account.

First consider **Operating Profit** - the measurement of local operating performance.

This was shown within the model as being:

PROFIT AND LOSS ACCOUNT

OPERATING PROFIT

ATTRIBUTABLE COSTS

The operating (or attributable) costs of the business result from two types of Revenue Expenditure:

Product-related: Those forming part of the product cost and ultimately the **cost of goods sold**

Expenses: Those which relate to the provision of support services, eg:
- selling
- distribution
- R & D
- personnel
- administration, etc

PROFIT AND LOSS ACCOUNT

OPERATING PROFIT
ATTRIBUTABLE COSTS

Whilst each company will have its own unique costing system, typically the division would be:

- **Product-related:** Material, parts purchased for re-sale, shopfloor labour, manufacturing expenses (ie: Production Overheads)

- **Expenses:** All non-manufacturing departmental running costs

The two categories are shown separately on the statement as:

- Cost of goods sold (Product-Related)

- Expenses (sometimes referred to as Support Services)

Product Costing systems are explained in *The Managing Budgets Pocketbook*.

PROFIT AND LOSS ACCOUNT

OPERATING PROFIT

Hence a more detailed statement of Operating Profit would show:

	£
Sales	1600
Less:	
Cost of goods sold	1000
Gross Profit	600
Less:	
Expenses	400
Operating Profit	200

Note:

1   Gross Profit is the difference between the selling price and the cost of manufacturing the goods sold in the period.

2   Operating Profit is the lowest level in the Profit and Loss Account over which operational management has control. (This is often referred to as PBIT ... Profit Before Interest and Tax or the 'Bottom Line').

PROFIT AND LOSS ACCOUNT

FINANCING COSTS

After accounting for the operating costs of the business there are other costs still to be met.

- **Interest:** Loan interest to be paid in accordance with the contractual agreement. p14

  Note - Interest must be paid whether the company has had a good year or not, so the greater the loan capital within the business, the greater the financial risk.

- **Tax:** Whilst businesses aim to minimise their tax bills by legitimate means (tax avoidance) the key determinant in the amount paid will be government fiscal policy.

The profits left over after allowing for Interest and Tax are called **Earnings.**

PROFIT AND LOSS ACCOUNT

EARNINGS

Earnings are what is left after all the business costs have been met.
Earnings, therefore, belong to the shareholders.

Some of the Earnings will be paid out to the shareholder to give them income on their investment. This is the **Dividend.**

The rest will be re-invested back within the business enabling the business to grow.
This is the **Retained Profit** and will be included on the Balance Sheet
as Reserves.   p54

PROFIT AND LOSS ACCOUNT

DIVIDEND PAYMENT

HOW MUCH DIVIDEND TO PAY

- Retained Profit is the cheapest form of Long-Term Finance, so most companies will wish to retain as much as possible
- But shareholders expect income as well as growth
- Failure to keep the shareholders happy can result in the removal of the Board of Directors and/or leave the company vulnerable to takeover bids ◀◀ p11

So the way Earnings are divided has to be a political decision.

Substantial shareholders, eg, financial institutions, will prefer a steady flow of dividend. Therefore, if Earnings fluctuate from year-to-year, so will Retained Profit.

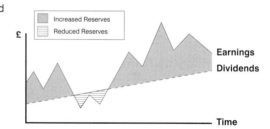

Legend:
- Increased Reserves
- Reduced Reserves

£

Earnings

Dividends

Time

(84) *Note that under certain conditions Dividends can even exceed Earnings - resulting in a reduction in Reserves.*

PROFIT AND LOSS ACCOUNT

EXAMPLE - ARC PLC

Profit and Loss Account for the 12 months ending 31st December 200-[1]

		£'000	£'000
	Sales		1,600
Less:	Cost of Goods Sold [2]		
	Direct Materials	500	
	Direct Labour	150	
	Production Overheads	350	
			1,000
	Gross Profit		600
Less:	**Expenses**		
	Administration	200	
	Selling	60	
	Distribution	80	
	Marketing	60	
	Total Expenses		400
	Net Operating Profit		200
Less:	**Interest**		33
	Net Profit Before Tax		167
Less:	**Tax**		57
	Earnings		110
Less:	**Dividend**		30
	Retained Profits		80

Note
1 The statement relates to the defined period of time for which the profits or losses are being measured.
2 Cost of Goods Sold is sometimes analysed into the different elements of product cost.

PROFIT AND LOSS ACCOUNT

COST OF GOODS SOLD

An alternative presentation of the Cost of Goods Sold is:

	£'000
Opening stock of Finished Goods	260
Add:	
Finished Goods completed during the period	920
	1,180
Less:	
Closing Stock of Finished Goods	180
Cost of Goods Sold	1,000

PROFIT AND LOSS ACCOUNT

COST OF GOODS SOLD

- Assume the company has a Finished Goods stock at the start of the period of £260k

- During the period £920k of completed products are transferred from production

- At the end of the period, if nothing had been sold, there would be £1,180k stock of Finished Goods

- However, when the closing stock is valued there is found to be only £180k in stock

- Hence, **by difference**, the value of stock shipped from Finished Goods, ie: the Cost of Goods Sold - must be £1,000k

PROFIT AND LOSS ACCOUNT

COMMON MISCONCEPTIONS

'If I compare the results of two businesses, the one which has made more profit has done better.'

*Not necessarily. What matters is not profit but profitability, ie: how much profit has been made on every £1 invested in the business. After all, if evaluating the opportunity to invest in a project offering a profit of £1,000 the first question would be: `How much has to be invested in order to make the £1,000 profit?' Company performance is measured on this basis using the **Return on Capital Employed (ROCE)***

$$ROCE = \frac{\textbf{Operating Profit}}{\textbf{Net Capital Employed}} \times 100$$

Note

- *Operating Profit is used as being the lowest level in the Profit and Loss Account over which operational management has control* *p81*

(88)
- *Net Capital Employed = Source of Funds* 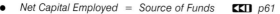 *p61*

PROFIT AND LOSS ACCOUNT

COMMON MISCONCEPTIONS

EXAMPLE

Compare the performance of companies X and Y:

	Operating Profit	Net Capital Employed	ROCE
	£m	£m	%
X	10	25	40
Y	100	400	25

Hence, although Y makes 10 times more operating profit than X, X is the better investment as it generates 40p per £1 long-term finance compared with Y's 25p.

PROFIT AND LOSS ACCOUNT

PUBLISHED FORMAT

The Profit and Loss Account

..... Published Format

A Report to the Business Owners

..... the Shareholders

PROFIT AND LOSS ACCOUNT

PUBLISHED FORMAT

- This report to the Shareholders is published and consequently is available to the competitors

  Consider the dilemma:
  - provide information to inform the Owners
  - competitors use published information

- Therefore the practice tends to be to provide the legal minimum in terms of specific numbers and to provide business statements and pictures to support the numbers shown (eg: the Directors' Report)

- Key items of Revenue Expenditure are given in the Notes to the Accounts, eg:
  - Payroll Costs; Payroll Expenses; Social Security Costs; Depreciation; Charitable Donations; Political Contributions, etc

PROFIT AND LOSS ACCOUNT

PUBLISHED FORMAT

- At first glance the format may not look dissimilar to the internal management format

- Preceding years' figures are required to be shown

- Figures shown are totals only - some analysis will be available in the Notes to the Accounts

- In large companies/groups it will be difficult, if not impossible, to break down the figures - by product, customer or business units

- The Published Statement is subject to audit

(Note: Special rules apply for small companies)

Profit and Loss Account for the 12 months ended...		
		£'000
	Turnover	1600
Less:	Operating Costs	1400
	Profit before Interest and Tax	200
Less:	Interest	33
	Profit before Tax	167
Less:	Tax	57
	Earnings	110
Less:	Dividend	30
	Retained Profits	80

APPENDIX ONE
JARGON EXPLAINED

APPENDIX ONE

JARGON EXPLAINED

APPENDIX ONE

JARGON EXPLAINED

APPENDIX ONE

JARGON EXPLAINED

		Page
Fixed Asset:	Facilities or Processes providing the infrastructure of the business. These are purchased for use within the business rather than for purposes of re-sale	19
Gross Profit:	**Sales** less **Cost of Goods Sold**	80
Interest:	Lenders will expect a return on their investment in the form of interest	30
Inventory:	See **Stock**	
Loan Capital:	Long Term investment in the business in the form of a loan	13
Net Assets Employed:	The accountant's expression for `**Use of Funds**', ie: **Fixed Assets** and **Working Capital**	61
Net Book Value:	Fixed Assets are valued at Net Book Value in the Balance Sheet, being Cost less Depreciation	46

APPENDIX ONE

JARGON EXPLAINED

		Page
Net Capital Employed:	The accountant's expression for \`**Source of Funds**', ie: **Net Worth** and **Loan Capital**	61
Net Profit:	See **Operating Profit**	
Net Worth:	See **Shareholders' Funds**	
Operating Profit:	A measure of local operating performance. This is the profit after all operating costs (product-related and expenses) have been considered, but before financing costs, eg: **Interest, Tax** and **Dividend**	78
Operating Statement:	See **Profit and Loss Account**	
Payables:	See **Creditors**	
Product Cost:	This will depend on the company's costing system but will typically include the cost of material, shopfloor labour and associated manufacturing expenses	80

JARGON EXPLAINED

		Page
Profit and Loss Account:	A financial statement measuring profit performance for a stated trading period	69
Receivables:	See **Debtors**	
Reserves:	A collective term for undistributed profits which form part of **Shareholders' Funds**. The principal reserves are: **Retained Profits, Share Premium Account** and **Revaluation Reserve**	54
Retained Profits:	Profits which are reinvested within the business	16
Revaluation Reserve:	On revaluing **Fixed Assets** any increase or decrease in value is matched by an increase or decrease in the Revaluation Reserve	55
Revenue Account:	See **Profit and Loss Account**	

APPENDIX ONE

JARGON EXPLAINED

		Page
Revenue Expenditure:	All expenditure which does not result in an increase in the value of Fixed Assets	36
ROCE:	Return on **Capital Employed**. Measures the effective use of **Net Capital Employed** to generate **Operating Profit**	88

$$= \frac{\text{Operating Profit}}{\text{Net Capital Employed}} \times 100$$

		Page
Sales:	The invoice value of goods sold (excluding VAT)	74
Share Capital:	Long-term funding by Shareholders who buy a share of the business ownership	10
Share Premium Account:	When shares are issued at a price above nominal value, the premiums are accumulated to form this **Reserve**	54

JARGON EXPLAINED

		Page
Shareholders' Funds:	The total shareholder investment in the business, ie: **Share Capital** and **Reserves**	60
Stock:	The total value of raw materials, work in progress and finished goods	21
Tax:	Part of company profits have to be used to finance the tax bill paid to the Government	81
Trading Account:	See **Profit and Loss Account**	
Turnover:	See **Sales**	
Working Capital:	Funds used to provide the flow of materials, services and credit. **(Current Assets - Current Liabilities)**	22
Written Down Value:	See **Net Book Value**	

APPENDIX TWO
CALCULATING DEPRECIATION

APPENDIX TWO

CALCULATING DEPRECIATION

How do accountants decide how much depreciation to charge?

Depreciation is .....

**Assessed on an annual basis by apportioning the
'depreciable amount' over the
'effective useful life'.**

CALCULATING DEPRECIATION

- What is the depreciable amount?

  That part of the Capital Expenditure which is 'consumed' by the business

  ie: Cost less residual/scrap value at the end of the asset's useful life to the business

CALCULATING DEPRECIATION

- What is the effective useful life?

  The period over which the business intends to use the Fixed Assets.

 40-50 years?

 3-5 years?

 4-25 years?

 2-5 years?

- How many years will it benefit the business?
  - how long will the asset last?
  - what is the likelihood of a breakthrough in technology?
  - and when would this happen?
  - what is the market life of the products requiring this facility?

The accountant may need some help deciding this!

CALCULATING DEPRECIATION

STRAIGHT-LINE METHOD

The most simple basis for apportioning the depreciable amount over the effective useful life is the `straight-line' method.

$$\frac{\text{Depreciable amount}}{\text{Useful life}}$$

= £ .... p.a.

Example:

A company purchases a new machine which costs £500,000 to make a product which has an expected life of 5 years. It is estimated that at the end of the 5 years the machine will have a resale value of £50,000.

Depreciation charge p.a.   = $\frac{\text{£500,000 - £50,000}}{\text{5 years}}$

= £90,000 p.a.

APPENDIX TWO

CALCULATING DEPRECIATION

OTHER METHODS

There are other methods of calculating depreciation, eg:

- **Reducing balance** - where the depreciation charge is a fixed % per annum of the reduced balance (ie: cost less cumulative depreciation)

- **Production Unit method** - where the depreciation charge depends on the number of units of output produced

Companies must select the method which is most appropriate to the asset in question and its application within the business.

The choice of method and the parameters used **MATTER.**

It affects - Profit
- Product Cost
- Fixed Asset Values

Don't let the accountant take sole responsibility!

About the Authors

Anne Hawkins, BA, ACMA is a Management Accountant with a first class honours degree in Business Studies. Anne has progressed from this strong knowledge base to gain senior management accounting experience within consumer and industrial product industries. As a Training Consultant she develops and presents finance programmes to Directors and Managers from all sections of industry.

Clive Turner, ACMA, MBCS is Managing Director of Structured Learning Programmes Ltd, established in 1981 to provide management consultancy and training services. Clive works with management to develop strategic business options. He participates in the evaluation process: designs the appropriate organisation structure and provides management development to support the implementation process. Clive continues to have extensive experience in delivering financial modules within Masters Programmes in the UK and overseas.

Contact

For details of support materials available to help trainers and managers run finance courses in-company, contact the authors at:

Anne   The Spinney, 27 Queens Road, Cheltenham GL50 2LX

Clive   Tall Trees, Barkers Lane, Wythall, West Midlands B47 6BS

© Anne Hawkins and Clive Turner 1995
This edition published in 1995 by Management Pocketbooks Ltd.
Laurel House, Station Approach, Alresford, Hants SO24 9JH, U.K.   Reprinted 1997, 1999, 2000, 2002, 2004.

Design, typesetting and graphics by **efex ltd**   Printed in U.K.   ISBN 1 870471 326

THE MANAGEMENT POCKETBOOK SERIES

Pocketbooks

Appraisals
Assertiveness
Balance Sheet
Business Planning
Business Presenter's
Business Writing
Career Transition
Challengers
Coaching
Communicator's
Controlling Absenteeism
Creative Manager's
C.R.M.
Cross-cultural Business
Cultural Gaffes
Customer Service
Decision-making
Developing People
Discipline
E-commerce
E-customer Care
Emotional Intelligence
Empowerment

Facilitator's
Handling Complaints
Icebreakers
Improving Efficiency
Improving Profitability
Induction
Influencing
International Trade
Interviewer's
I.T. Trainer's
Key Account Manager's
Leadership
Learner's
Manager's
Managing Budgets
Managing Cashflow
Managing Change
Managing Upwards
Managing Your Appraisal
Marketing
Meetings
Mentoring
Motivation

Negotiator's
Networking
People Manager's
Performance Management
Personal Success
Project Management
Problem Behaviour
Problem Solving
Quality
Resolving Conflict
Sales Excellence
Salesperson's
Self-managed Development
Starting In Management
Stress
Teamworking
Telephone Skills
Telesales
Thinker's
Time Management
Trainer Standards
Trainer's

Pocketsquares

Great Presentation Scandal
Great Training Robbery
Hook Your Audience
Leadership: Sharing The Passion

Pocketfiles

Trainer's Blue Pocketfile of
Ready-to-use Exercises

Trainer's Green Pocketfile of
Ready-to-use Exercises

Trainer's Red Pocketfile of
Ready-to-use Exercises

ORDER FORM

No. copies

Your details

Name _____

Position _____

Company _____

Address _____

_____

_____

Telephone _____

Facsimile _____

E-mail _____

VAT No. (EC companies) _____

Your Order Ref _____

Please send me:

The Balance Sheet _____ Pocketbook ☐

The _____ Pocketbook ☐

The _____ Pocketbook ☐

The _____ Pocketbook ☐

The _____ Pocketbook ☐

Order by Post
MANAGEMENT POCKETBOOKS LTD
LAUREL HOUSE, STATION APPROACH, ALRESFORD,
HAMPSHIRE SO24 9JH UK

Order by Phone, Fax or Internet
Telephone: +44 (0)1962 735573
Facsimile: +44 (0)1962 733637
E-mail: sales@pocketbook.co.uk
Web: www.pocketbook.co.uk

Customers in USA should contact:
Stylus Publishing, LLC, 22883 Quicksilver Drive,
Sterling, VA 20166-2012
Telephone: 703 661 1581 or 800 232 0223
Facsimile: 703 661 1501 E-mail: styluspub@aol.com